D1069051

STATE PROFILES

NORTH CAROLINA

BY NATHAN SOMMER

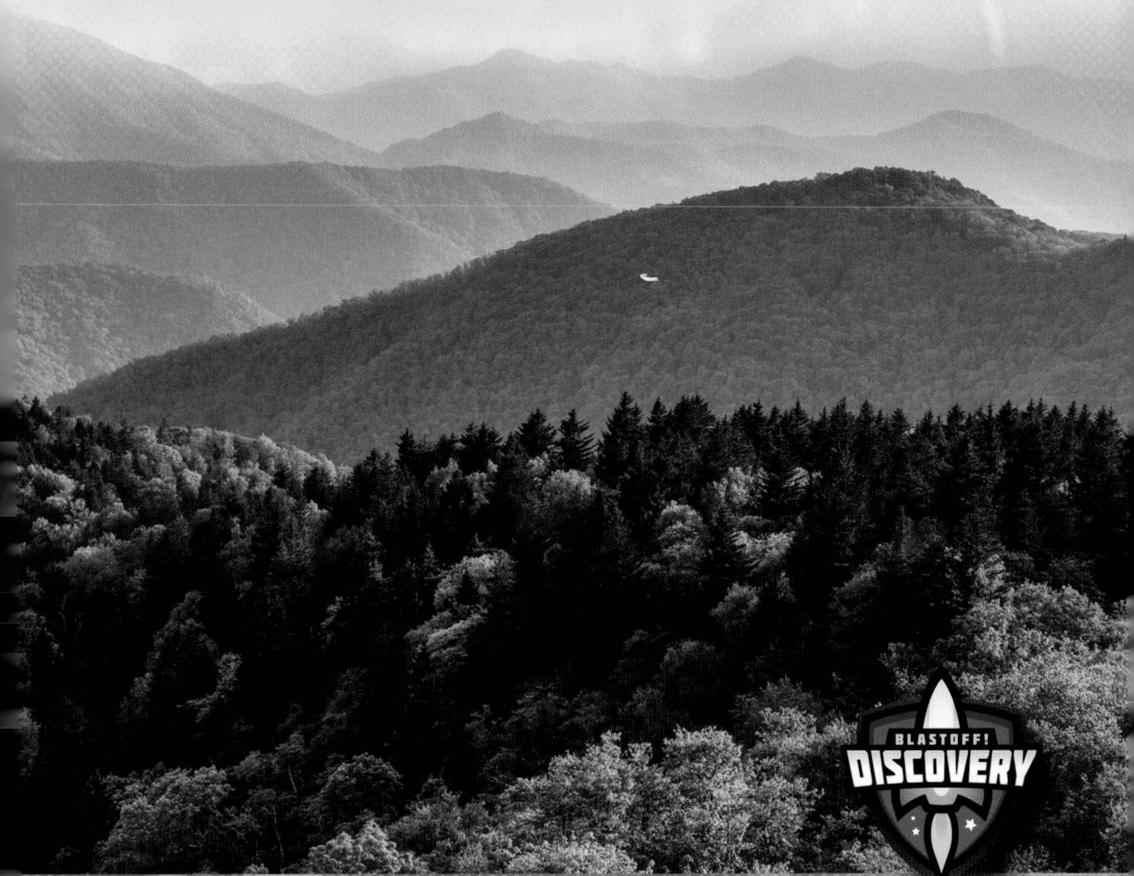

BLASTOFF! DISCOVERY

BELLWETHER MEDIA • MINNEAPOLIS, MN

Blastoff! Discovery launches a new mission: reading to learn. Filled with facts and features, each book offers you an exciting new world to explore!

This edition first published in 2022 by Bellwether Media, Inc.

No part of this publication may be reproduced in whole or in part without written permission of the publisher.
For information regarding permission, write to Bellwether Media, Inc., Attention: Permissions Department,
6012 Blue Circle Drive, Minnetonka, MN 55343.

Library of Congress Cataloging-in-Publication Data

Names: Sommer, Nathan, author.
Title: North Carolina / Nathan Sommer.
Description: Minneapolis, MN : Bellwether Media, 2022. |
    Series: Blastoff! Discovery: State profiles | Includes bibliographical
    references and index. | Audience: Ages 7-13 | Audience: Grades
    4-6 | Summary: "Engaging images accompany information about
    North Carolina. The combination of high-interest subject matter and
    narrative text is intended for students in grades 3 through 8"–
    Provided by publisher.
Identifiers: LCCN 2021020868 (print) | LCCN 2021020869 (ebook)
    | ISBN 9781644873380 (library binding) |
    ISBN 9781648341816 (ebook)
Subjects: LCSH: North Carolina–Juvenile literature.
Classification: LCC F254.3 .S66 2021 (print) | LCC F254.3 (ebook)
    | DDC 975.6–dc23
LC record available at https://lccn.loc.gov/2021020868
LC ebook record available at https://lccn.loc.gov/2021020869

Text copyright © 2022 by Bellwether Media, Inc. BLASTOFF!
DISCOVERY and associated logos are trademarks and/or registered
trademarks of Bellwether Media, Inc.

Editor: Colleen Sexton   Designer: Laura Sowers

Printed in the United States of America, North Mankato, MN.

TABLE OF CONTENTS

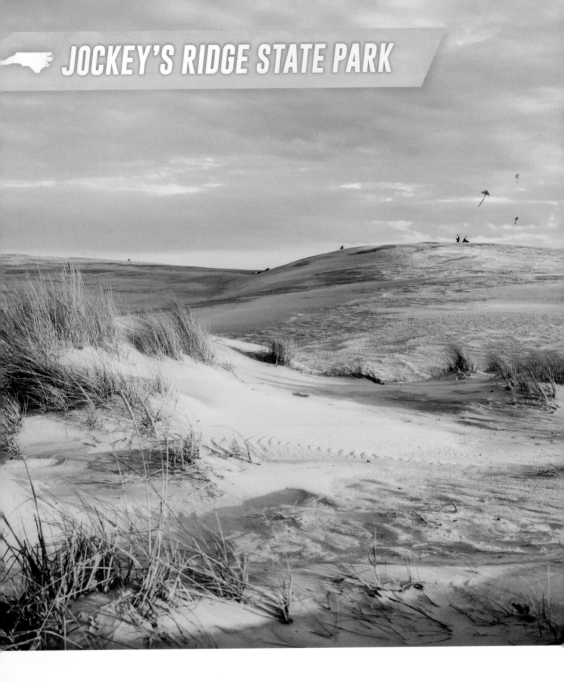

A family arrives at Jockey's Ridge State Park in Nags Head. A view of the Atlantic Ocean greets them. It glitters just beyond towering white sand **dunes**. Some dunes are bigger than a house! The tallest reach 100 feet (30 meters) tall.

BILTMORE ESTATE

CAPE HATTERAS LIGHTHOUSE

CHIMNEY ROCK

GRANDFATHER MOUNTAIN

The family spots sandboarders surfing down the sandy slopes. They look up to see hang gliders flying high overhead. Farther along, dozens of colorful kites fill the sky. Which adventure will the family choose first? Their journey in North Carolina has just begun!

North Carolina is in the southeastern United States. The Atlantic Ocean meets the state's long eastern border. South Carolina lies to the south. A small corner of the state touches Georgia in the southwest. Tennessee is North Carolina's western neighbor. Virginia sits to the north.

North Carolina covers 53,819 square miles (139,391 square kilometers). Raleigh is the capital. It lies in the middle of the state. The most populated city is Charlotte. It stands near the Catawba River and Lake Norman, one of the state's largest lakes. Other major cities include Greensboro, Winston-Salem, Durham, and Fayetteville.

KENTUCKY

TENNESSEE

GEORGIA

WEST VIRGINIA

VIRGINIA

GREENSBORO

WINSTON-SALEM

DURHAM

RALEIGH

CATAWBA RIVER

NORTH CAROLINA

CHARLOTTE

FAYETTEVILLE

SOUTH CAROLINA

ATLANTIC OCEAN

IT'S A PLAN!

Raleigh is the only state capital in the country to be planned. It was named North Carolina's state capital before it was even built!

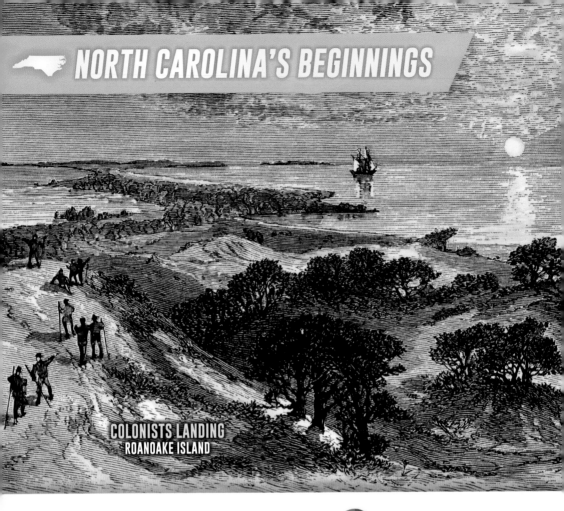

COLONISTS LANDING ROANOAKE ISLAND

People first arrived in North Carolina about 12,000 years ago. Over time, they formed Native American tribes. They included the Catawba, Cherokee, and Tuscarora. The Spanish and French explored North Carolina's shores in the 1500s. Roanoke Island became the area's first English **settlement** in 1585.

THE LOST COLONY

The 115 people of the Roanoke Island settlement disappeared. They were never seen again. To this day, no one knows for sure what happened to them.

North Carolina became 1 of 13 English **colonies**. The colonies fought the **Revolutionary War** and won their independence. In 1789, North Carolina became the 12th state. By 1800, the population included about 140,000 Black people. Most were **enslaved** on small farms. North Carolina fought for the South during the **Civil War**.

NATIVE PEOPLES OF NORTH CAROLINA

EASTERN BAND OF CHEROKEE INDIANS

- Original Cherokee lands in North Carolina, Alabama, Georgia, and Tennessee
- Eastern Band formed by those who escaped when the U.S. government forced the Cherokee to move west in 1838
- About 14,000 live in North Carolina today

LUMBEE TRIBE

- Original lands in south-central North Carolina around the Lumbee River
- About 55,000 live in North Carolina today
- Largest tribe east of the Mississippi River

North Carolina's landscape slopes upward from east to west. **Barrier islands** called the Outer Banks line the coast. Marshlands, lakes, and swamps cover the Atlantic Coastal **Plain** in eastern North Carolina. Part of the Great Dismal Swamp lies in this region. Low hills roll across the Piedmont **Plateau** in central North Carolina. In the west, the land rises to the Blue Ridge and Great Smoky Mountains. These ranges are part of the Appalachian Mountains.

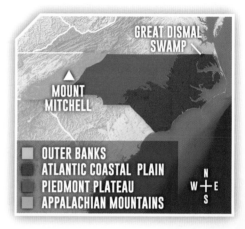

GREAT DISMAL SWAMP

MOUNT MITCHELL

- OUTER BANKS
- ATLANTIC COASTAL PLAIN
- PIEDMONT PLATEAU
- APPALACHIAN MOUNTAINS

N
W +E
S

GREAT DISMAL SWAMP

BLUE RIDGE MOUNTAINS

SPRING
HIGH: 70°F (21°C)
LOW: 51°F (11°C)

SUMMER
HIGH: 86°F (30°C)
LOW: 67°F (19°C)

FALL
HIGH: 72°F (22°C)
LOW: 52°F (11°C)

WINTER
HIGH: 53°F (12°C)
LOW: 34°F (1°C)

°F = degrees Fahrenheit
°C = degrees Celsius

NORTH CAROLINA'S CHALLENGE: CLIMATE CHANGE

North Carolina's sea level is rising about 1 inch (2.5 centimeters) every two years. Some areas lose up to 10 feet (3 meters) of coastline each year. This wearing away of the land costs billions of dollars in damage.

North Carolina has hot, muggy summers. Winters are mild. The west is cooler and drier than the east. **Hurricanes** bring damaging winds and flooding to coastal residents.

THE HIGHEST PEAK

Mount Mitchell is the highest peak east of the Mississippi River. It stands 6,684 feet (2,037 meters) above sea level.

North Carolina supports a variety of wildlife. Blue marlins, sailfish, and dolphinfish swim in coastal waters. Diamondback rattlesnakes slither across the sandy coastal plains. Otters, beavers, and alligators live in wetlands. There, turtles and salamanders watch out for cottonmouth snakes. The wetlands are also a stopover for ducks, snow geese, and other **migrating** birds.

Forests are home to foxes, opossums, and skunks. Cardinals, wrens, and mockingbirds sing from the trees. Black bears, elk, and coyotes roam the Appalachian Mountains. Golden eagles and barn owls snatch up small prey in mountain forests.

SNOW GOOSE

BLACK BEAR

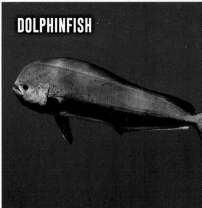

DOLPHINFISH

BARN OWL

RED FOX

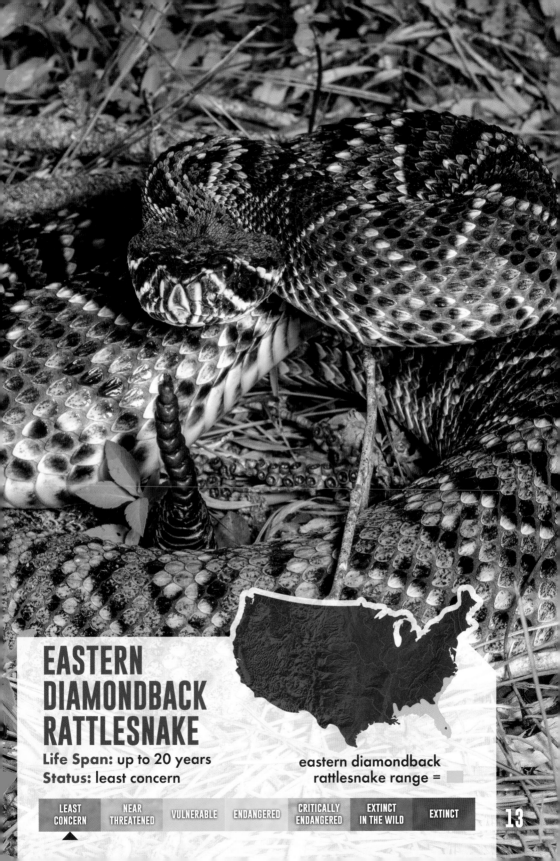

EASTERN DIAMONDBACK RATTLESNAKE

Life Span: up to 20 years
Status: least concern

eastern diamondback
rattlesnake range =

LEAST CONCERN	NEAR THREATENED	VULNERABLE	ENDANGERED	CRITICALLY ENDANGERED	EXTINCT IN THE WILD	EXTINCT

More than 10.4 million people call North Carolina home. About three in four live in **urban** areas. The state has nine cities with more than 100,000 people. Most **rural** residents live in small towns.

NORTH CAROLINA'S CHALLENGE: RURAL COMMUNITIES

North Carolina's cities receive more money for education and technology than rural areas. Young people often leave rural areas for better education and career opportunities in cities. With fewer career options, the rural workforce is more likely to suffer from poverty.

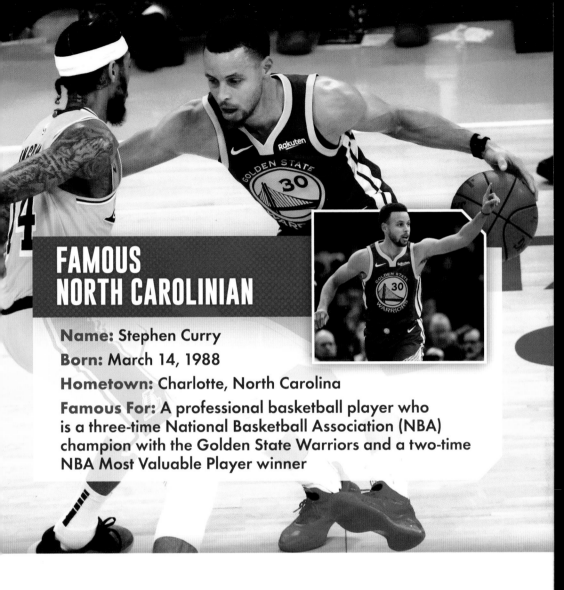

FAMOUS NORTH CAROLINIAN

Name: Stephen Curry

Born: March 14, 1988

Hometown: Charlotte, North Carolina

Famous For: A professional basketball player who is a three-time National Basketball Association (NBA) champion with the Golden State Warriors and a two-time NBA Most Valuable Player winner

Most North Carolinians have **ancestors** from England, Scotland, Germany, and other European countries. Black or African Americans make up about one-fifth of the population. The state has the largest Native American population east of the Mississippi River. The Lumbee of southern North Carolina is the largest tribe. Small numbers of North Carolinians are Asian American or Hispanic. Many **immigrants** come from Mexico, India, Honduras, China, and El Salvador.

Scottish, Irish, and German farmers founded Charlotte in 1768. The nearby Catawba River made Charlotte an important trading port. Later, it became a center for the gold mining and **textile** industries.

Today, Charlotte is North Carolina's largest city. Dozens of skyscrapers stand downtown. Many of the country's major banks are based there. The Daniel Stowe Botanical Garden and Freedom Park are favorite gathering places. Residents walk and bike the Little Sugar Creek Greenway. Visitors check out the Discovery Place Science museum and the NASCAR Hall of Fame. The Mint Museum draws art lovers.

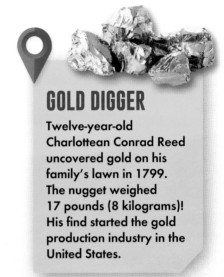

GOLD DIGGER

Twelve-year-old Charlottean Conrad Reed uncovered gold on his family's lawn in 1799. The nugget weighed 17 pounds (8 kilograms)! His find started the gold production industry in the United States.

FREEDOM PARK

TOBACCO FIELD

North Carolina's early economy depended on growing tobacco and cotton. Today, farmland covers one-fourth of the state. North Carolina remains the nation's top tobacco producer. Farmers also raise hogs, chickens, and turkeys. Off the coast, fishing crews haul in blue crabs, shrimp, and tuna.

THE RESEARCH TRIANGLE

The cities of Raleigh, Durham, and Chapel Hill are nicknamed the Research Triangle. The area is known for its technology and medical companies.

North Carolina's thick forests provide lumber. The state leads the nation in making furniture. Factory workers also create textiles and produce computer products. Most North Carolinians have **service jobs**. They work in schools, hospitals, and restaurants. Banking is one of the state's largest service industries. The state's military bases also employ many workers.

INVENTED IN NORTH CAROLINA

VICKS VAPORUB
Date Invented: 1894
Inventor: Lunsford Richardson

FIRST SUCCESSFUL AIRPLANE
Date Invented: 1903
Inventors: Wilbur and Orville Wright

PEPSI
Date Invented: 1893
Inventor: Caleb Bradham

KRISPY KREME DOUGHNUTS
Date Invented: 1937
Inventor: Vernon Rudolph

SHRIMP AND GRITS

North Carolinians eat fresh seafood from coastal waters. Fish stew mixes sheepshead, bacon, and potatoes in a warm tomato broth. Cooks serve shrimp and grits for breakfast, lunch, and dinner. They heat ground corn with milk and butter and cover it with sweet shrimp.

SO MANY SWEET POTATOES

North Carolina's state vegetable is the sweet potato. Farmers grow more than half of the country's sweet potatoes. This crop grows easily in the state's rich soil and warm climate.

North Carolina is also famous for its smoky pork barbecue. Residents eat pulled pork sandwiches and hot dogs "Carolina-style" topped with crunchy coleslaw and onions. Popular side dishes include hush puppies and fried green tomatoes with pimento cheese. North Carolinians enjoy peach cobbler made with home-grown peaches. Sweet potato pie is another favorite dessert.

CAROLINA-STYLE BARBECUE

HUSH PUPPIES

4-6 SERVINGS

Have an adult help you make this tasty side!

INGREDIENTS

1/2 cup flour
1/2 cup yellow cornmeal
1/2 teaspoon salt
1/4 teaspoon baking soda
1/2 teaspoon black pepper

1 large egg
1/2 cup buttermilk
1/4 cup minced onion
2 cups vegetable oil for frying

DIRECTIONS

1. Combine the first five ingredients in a bowl.
2. Stir together the egg and buttermilk and add to the dry ingredients.
3. Stir until just moistened, and then stir in the onion.
4. Pour the oil into a large, heavy frying pan. Heat to 375 degrees Fahrenheit (191 degrees Celsius).
5. Carefully drop the batter by tablespoonfuls into the oil. Fry in small batches for 3 minutes on each side or until golden.
6. Drain on paper towels and serve immediately.

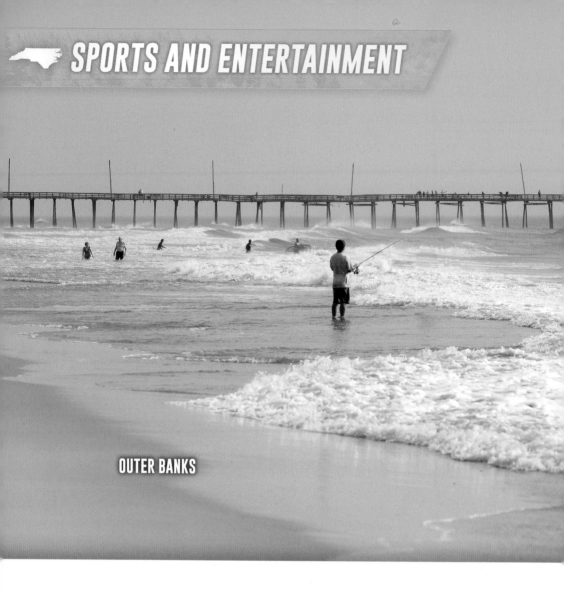

OUTER BANKS

North Carolinians enjoy the outdoors. They hike and camp in Great Smoky Mountains National Park. Locals in the Outer Banks head to beaches to paddleboard, fish, and kayak. Art galleries and museums draw many visitors. Residents explore the past at the North Carolina Museum of History. The North Carolina Symphony performs throughout the state.

Sports fans cheer for the state's professional football, basketball, and hockey teams. College sports are also popular. Crowds fill the stands for Duke University basketball games. Millions watch NASCAR races at the Charlotte Motor Speedway each year.

DUKE UNIVERSITY BASKETBALL

NOTABLE SPORTS TEAM

Carolina Panthers
Sport: National Football League
Started: 1993
Place of Play: Bank of America Stadium

**GRANDFATHER MOUNTAIN
HIGHLAND GAMES**

128

North Carolinians share their **culture** during festivals. Each July, the Grandfather Mountain Highland Games celebrate the state's Scottish **heritage**. Residents play games and watch **Celtic** music performances. In October, the Homegrown Music Fest in Dorton honors North Carolina's musical roots. More than 100 acts play **bluegrass**, blues, and jazz.

Residents also come together for community celebrations. Mount Olive's North Carolina Pickle Festival in April features a pickle-eating contest. Every October, colorful kites fill the sky at the Carolina Kite Fest in Atlantic Beach. Wilmington Riverfest welcomes visitors each October with craft stalls, concerts, and fireworks. North Carolinians have plenty of options for fun!

WATER CYCLING

Every Fourth of July, the coastal town of Beaufort hosts an underwater bike race. Racers decorate their bikes. Then they put on scuba gear and pedal or push their bikes to the finish line!

CAROLINA KITE FEST

1712

The Carolina Colony splits into North Carolina and South Carolina

1524

Italian explorer Giovanni da Verrazzano maps North Carolina's coast, becoming the first European to explore the area

1789

North Carolina becomes the 12th state

1585

Roanoke Island becomes the area's first English settlement

1830

The U.S. government forces Native Americans to leave North Carolina and move west

1861

North Carolina leaves the United States to fight in the Civil War for the South

1960

Four young Black men protest racial segregation at a lunch counter in Greensboro, leading to sit-in protests nationwide

1868

North Carolina rejoins the United States

2016

Protests erupt in Charlotte after the police-related death of Keith Lamont Scott

1903

The Wright brothers complete the first airplane flight at Kitty Hawk

NORTH CAROLINA FACTS

Nickname: The Tar Heel State

Motto: *Esse Quam Videri* (To Be, Rather Than to Seem)

Date of Statehood: November 21, 1789
(the 12th state)

Capital City: Raleigh ★

Other Major Cities: Charlotte, Greensboro, Winston-Salem, Durham, Fayetteville

Area: 53,819 square miles (139,391 square kilometers); North Carolina is the 28th largest state.

Population

10,439,388
(2020)

STATE FLAG

North Carolina's state flag was adopted in 1885. The flag has a vertical blue stripe on the left and horizontal stripes, one red and one white, on the right. The blue stripe features a white star between the letters N and C. A banner above the star reads "May 20th 1775" and a banner below reads "April 12th 1776." Both dates represent North Carolina declaring its independence from Great Britain.

INDUSTRY

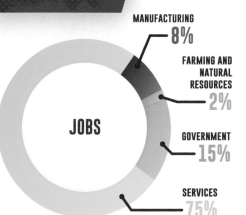

JOBS

MANUFACTURING
8%

FARMING AND
NATURAL
RESOURCES
2%

GOVERNMENT
15%

SERVICES
75%

Main Exports

machinery

tobacco

chemicals

furniture

Natural Resources
granite, clay, gravel, sand, forests

GOVERNMENT

Federal Government

14 | **2**
REPRESENTATIVES | SENATORS

USA

NC

16
ELECTORAL
VOTES

State Government

120 | **50**
REPRESENTATIVES | SENATORS

STATE SYMBOLS

STATE BIRD
NORTHERN CARDINAL

STATE ANIMAL
GRAY SQUIRREL

STATE FLOWER
FLOWERING DOGWOOD

STATE TREE
PINE

GLOSSARY

ancestors—relatives who lived long ago

barrier islands—long, sandy islands along a shore created by wind and waves

bluegrass—a style of music played on string instruments; bluegrass began in the southern Appalachian region of the United States.

Celtic—relating to the language and culture of Scottish and Irish people

Civil War—a war between the Northern (Union) and Southern (Confederate) states that lasted from 1861 to 1865

colonies—distant territories under the control of another nation

culture—the beliefs, arts, and ways of life in a place or society

dunes—hills of sand

enslaved—considered property and forced to work for no pay

heritage—the traditions, achievements, and beliefs that are part of the history of a group of people

hurricanes—storms formed in the tropics that have violent winds and often have rain and lightning

immigrants—people who move to a new country

migrating—traveling from one place to another, often with the seasons

plain—a large area of flat land

plateau—an area of flat, raised land

Revolutionary War—the war from 1775 to 1783 in which the United States fought for independence from Great Britain

rural—related to the countryside

service jobs—jobs that perform tasks for people or businesses

settlement—a place where newly arrived people live

textile—woven or knitted cloth

urban—related to cities or city life

AT THE LIBRARY

The Civil War Visual Encyclopedia. New York, N.Y.: DK Children, 2021.

Loh-Hagan, Virginia. *Roanoke Colony.* Ann Arbor, Mich.: 45th Parallel Press, 2018.

Squire, Ann O. *North Carolina.* New York, N.Y.: Children's Press, 2018.

ON THE WEB

FACTSURFER

Factsurfer.com gives you a safe, fun way to find more information.

1. Go to www.factsurfer.com.

2. Enter "North Carolina" into the search box and click 🔍.

3. Select your book cover to see a list of related content.

INDEX

The images in this book are reproduced through the courtesy of: jadimages, front cover, pp. 2-3; James R. Martin, p. 3; J Paulson/ Alamy, pp. 4-5; Konstantin L, p. 5 (Biltmore Estate); Pi-Lens, p. 5 (Cape Hatteras Lighthouse); Chad Coble, p. 5 (Chimney Rock); Jon Bilous, pp. 5 (Grandfather Mountain), 26-32 (background); North Wind Picture Archives/ Alamy, p. 8; Bryant, William Cullen, Gay, Sydney Howard/ Wikipedia, p. 8 (Roanoke); anthony heflin, p. 9; fStop Images GmbH/ Alamy, p. 10; Dave Allen Photography, p. 11 (Blue Ridge Mountains); Paul Brady Photography, p. 11 (inset); Roy E Farr, p. 11 (Mount Mitchell); Michael Shake, p. 12 (barn owl); Double Brow Imagergy, p. 12 (snow goose); emperorcorsar, p. 12 (black bear); FtLaud, p. 12 (dolphinfish); Sandra Standbridge, p. 12 (red fox); George Grall/ Alamy, p. 13 (rattlesnake); Nolichuckyjake, p. 14; ZUMA Press/ Alamy, pp. 15, 23 (Duke); Tribune Content Agency LLC/ Alamy, p. 15 (inset); Sean Pavone, p. 16; macrowildlife, p. 17 (gold); cpaulfell, p. 17; Johnnie Laws, p. 18; Eric Glenn, p. 19 (Vicks); vengerof, p. 19 (Pepsi); J J Osuna, p. 19 (airplane); Duplass, p. 19 (Krispy Kreme); Tom Worsley, p. 19; Natallya Naumava, p. 20 (shrimp and grits); Tiger Images, p. 20 (sweet potatoes); Jeremy Pawlowski, p. 21 (barbecue); Dennis Wildberger, p. 21 (hush puppy plate); bonchan, p. 21 (hush puppies); Anne Kitzman, p. 22; Grindstone Media Group, p. 23 (Carolina Panthers); Mtsaride, p. 23 (football); REUTERS/ Alamy, p. 24; Dave Hilbert, p. 25; F. Allegrini/ Wikipedia, p. 26 (da Verrazzano); imageBROKER/ Alamy, p. 26 (Roanoke); John T. Daniels/ Wikipedia, p. 27 (Wright Brothers); Millenius, p. 28 (flag); Connie Barr, p. 29 (cardinal); Giedriius, p. 29 (squirrel); Joy Brown, p. 29 (dogwood); Woodlot, p. 29 (pine); ThePhotoFab, p. 31.